I0012303

1. Introduction – The Evolving World of Excel Automation

For decades, Microsoft Excel has served as both a data tool and a quiet programming environment, empowering millions of users to automate calculations, reports, and workflows through the use of Visual Basic for Applications (VBA). Introduced in the 1990s, VBA quickly became a cornerstone of Office automation, offering power users and developers alike a way to transform spreadsheets from static grids into living, breathing tools that respond to input, manage complexity, and save time. In countless organizations, VBA scripts have powered financial models, inventory trackers, HR dashboards, and just about every flavour of business solution imaginable.

Yet in recent years, the landscape has started to shift. As cloud computing became more central to how teams collaborate and businesses operate, a growing number of companies began to move their work into browser-based environments. This transformation brought new challenges—and new opportunities—for Excel automation. The traditional model of relying solely on desktop-bound macros began to show its limits. Teams needed ways to share, run, and manage automations in real-time across locations and devices, without being tied to a single workstation or dealing with outdated local files. The future of Office automation had to be more connected, more collaborative, and more accessible.

In response to this evolution, Microsoft introduced **Office Scripts**, a cloud-first automation platform for Excel on the web. Office Scripts is not just a replacement for VBA—it's a reimagining of what automation can look like in the modern, online workspace. Built on TypeScript, Office Scripts offers the structure of a modern programming language with all the flexibility users have come to expect from Excel. It runs in the browser, lives in the Microsoft 365 cloud, and integrates seamlessly with other services like Power Automate, SharePoint, and Teams. Most importantly, it allows automations to move with the user—accessible from anywhere, sharable across the organization, and adaptable to the needs of both individuals and teams.

Still, while Office Scripts points toward the future, VBA remains deeply embedded in the present. Across industries, VBA continues to power mission-critical workflows. Many businesses have spent years developing complex, highly customized macros that are simply too valuable—and too embedded—to discard overnight. Moreover, Excel Desktop still offers features and user interface elements that the web version does not yet fully replicate. For this reason, mastering both VBA and Office Scripts is no longer just an advantage—it's a necessity for those looking to build flexible, future-ready automation solutions.

By understanding both platforms, developers and power users gain the freedom to design solutions that bridge the best of both worlds. They can maintain and optimize existing VBA systems while also experimenting with cloud-native tools that scale across teams and integrate with modern services. In the chapters ahead, this book will guide you through that journey—starting with a deeper dive into the differences between these two approaches, helping you understand when to use VBA, when to reach for Office Scripts, and when to blend them for maximum impact.

So let's begin with the question that's on many minds: **Excel VBA vs. Office Scripts—when should you use which?**

2. Excel VBA vs. Office Scripts: When to Use Which

Excel VBA has been a cornerstone of process automation for many years, empowering users to transform their spreadsheets into dynamic tools that handle everything from simple data manipulations to complex business workflows. Its robust capabilities, combined with the familiarity of the Visual Basic for Applications language, have made it a go-to choice for countless organizations, especially those that rely on legacy solutions. VBA scripts run best on the desktop version of Excel, tapping into a rich set of functionalities that cater to advanced data handling and user interface customizations. Over time, though, the world of work has expanded beyond individual machines and local networks, pushing developers to explore more agile, cloud-friendly solutions.

Office Scripts emerged to address the evolving needs of modern businesses, allowing Excel users to automate tasks right within their browser through Excel for the web. Built on TypeScript or JavaScript, Office Scripts provide a cross-platform approach that transcends the limitations of desktop environments. This means that wherever you can access Excel online, you can create, run, and share scripts without traditional installation hurdles or version conflicts. Instead of relying on purely local resources, you tap into Microsoft's cloud ecosystem, making the automation experience more collaborative and adaptable to remote work scenarios.

An important distinction lies in how each technology aligns with cross-platform requirements. VBA macros are strongly tied to Windows-based versions of Excel, a history that has long influenced how organizations structure their automation strategies. Office Scripts, by contrast, extend native script execution to a wide range of devices and operating systems, further enhancing how teams can collaborate on shared spreadsheets. This ability to script on virtually any device with internet access allows for more flexible business processes, particularly in enterprises that need solutions to work seamlessly across different offices and regions.

Office Scripts also integrate closely with tools like Power Automate. The cloud-based approach opens doors to event-driven workflows, connecting your Excel processes to countless other apps and services. This means you can trigger your Excel scripts when an email arrives, when a file is added to SharePoint, or when a specific condition is met within another part of your ecosystem. While VBA also supports event-driven procedures, its desktop-bound nature makes it more challenging to bridge these processes with external web services or modern APIs at a large scale. With Office Scripts, those integrations are built directly into Microsoft 365, offering a more native feel for cloud-based automation.

Deciding which approach to use depends on a balance of current needs, legacy dependencies, and future ambitions. Some organizations benefit from the deep roots of VBA and the wealth of existing code that has been refined for their business processes. Others prefer the cloud-first model of Office Scripts, which pairs well with a highly distributed workforce and the agility demands of modern data environments. In many cases, teams find themselves relying on a hybrid approach, retaining legacy VBA for mission-critical operations while slowly introducing Office Scripts to capitalize on the benefits of integrated cloud services.

When considering how to move forward, it is helpful to look at your broader ecosystem, the user community within your organization, and the long-term plan for digital transformation. VBA still holds considerable power for those with a locally centered approach to Excel, but Office Scripts point the way to a more interconnected future. The choice is not always absolute; many organizations run both systems concurrently, allowing them to capture the best of each world while gradually transitioning to newer technologies.

As we continue on our journey, the next natural step is to explore how to set up the development environment for these scripting solutions. By understanding the tools and configurations required, you will be able to fully leverage both VBA and Office Scripts in a seamless way. In the following chapter, "Setting Up Your Development Environment," we will explore the software installations, accounts, and best practices that enable effective and efficient Excel automation.

3. Setting Up Your Development Environment

Before diving into automating your spreadsheets and building sophisticated solutions, it is crucial to set up your development environment in a way that supports both VBA and Office Scripts. This dual approach allows you to work with traditional Excel desktop macros and modern, cloud-based scripts without interruptions, letting you seamlessly switch between projects as needed. Configuring the VBA editor for productivity involves a few considerations, such as enabling the Developer tab in Excel, adjusting settings in the Visual Basic Editor, and ensuring that you have the proper references for the libraries you plan to use. By taking time to familiarize yourself with the available debugging tools, layout options, and code navigation features, you can accelerate your coding speed and reduce common errors.

Office Scripts, on the other hand, require an environment that extends beyond your local machine. To begin, you need an Office 365 subscription that includes access to Excel for the web, along with the necessary permissions within your organization. Once those prerequisites are met, you can access the Office Scripts Code Editor through the Automate tab in Excel Online. This integrated browser-based editor provides an intuitive way to create, modify, and run your scripts without installing or configuring additional software. The convenience of working entirely online pairs well with a cloud-first mindset, encouraging you to store files in OneDrive or SharePoint and share them easily with colleagues.

For a smooth workflow, it helps to think about the nature of each project you undertake. When creating VBA macros for desktop-bound tasks and offline work, you might focus on leveraging existing libraries and crafting user interfaces with

Forms. When coding Office Scripts for web-based collaboration, you might emphasize how quickly you can deploy changes to multiple users in real time. Regardless of which environment you are in, consistency in naming conventions, clear file organization, and thorough documentation will reduce the potential for confusion and keep your projects on track. Because both VBA and Office Scripts have distinctive capabilities, managing their coexistence in your development environment will empower you to tackle a broad range of challenges.

One of the most important aspects of a fluid experience is knowing where to keep your core files, libraries, and references. If you are working locally, backing up your VBA modules in a safe repository is essential. If you are working online, check that your OneDrive or SharePoint folders are well-structured and that you have sufficient permissions to create and edit scripts. In many cases, you will also want to confirm that your organization's policies align with these development practices, particularly if your code interacts with sensitive data or third-party integrations.

After setting up your environment, you are ready to explore the best methods for creating, collaborating on, and maintaining your automated solutions. In the next chapter, "Best Practices for Collaborative Macro Development," we will delve into strategies for version control and coordination in team settings, covering everything from exporting VBA modules to SharePoint or Git to sharing Office Scripts with colleagues. We will also look at naming conventions and documentation standards that help keep your codebase manageable and your solutions running smoothly.

4. Best Practices for Collaborative Macro Development

Building and maintaining Excel macros in a collaborative environment requires careful coordination, version control, and clear communication among team members. When multiple developers or stakeholders are working on the same solution, it is easy for small changes to escalate into complicated overlaps and conflicts. One of the best ways to maintain consistency is to adopt a reliable version control process. Whether you choose a platform like Git or rely on SharePoint for document management, having a single source of truth helps you keep track of revisions and makes it easier to roll back unintended changes. Exporting your VBA modules periodically and storing them in a central repository allows team members to access the latest code and maintain a clear history of modifications and updates.

When collaborating on VBA code, it is helpful to establish a naming convention that clearly identifies the purpose of each module, procedure, or function. Descriptive and consistent names reduce confusion, especially when new developers join the project. It also helps to keep your directory structure tidy, with related scripts grouped together to make navigation more intuitive. Documenting your solutions as you build them is just as important as the code itself. Consider adding concise comments to highlight the purpose of each procedure, the variables it uses, and any dependencies on external libraries or resources. By dedicating the time to write this information, you create a living record that anyone can follow, which is particularly useful when deadlines are tight or when the team experiences turnover.

Sharing Office Scripts for Excel Online involves a similar mindset but operates within Microsoft 365's ecosystem. Storing these scripts in the cloud through OneDrive or SharePoint can make them instantly available to colleagues, who can copy, adapt, or extend your code for their own needs. Inviting others to collaborate in real time provides a smoother development experience because changes appear almost immediately. This level of transparency is especially valuable for geographically dispersed teams that depend on asynchronous collaboration. Using clear file names and thorough internal documentation further ensures that your scripts remain manageable over time. Although TypeScript or JavaScript might differ from VBA in style, the core principles of version control, good naming practices, and solid documentation remain the same.

Keeping an eye on how your team interacts with each macro is essential for continuous improvement. By gathering feedback and maintaining open lines of communication, you can refine your processes and add new features or fix bugs as required. This feedback loop is greatly facilitated by using common repositories or dedicated channels that allow you to track issues and suggestions. Over time, you may find yourself with a codebase that includes both VBA and Office Scripts, each complementing the other's strengths while serving diverse business needs. The goal is always to make sure that everyone involved can contribute without stepping on each other's toes, and that the final product is both robust and easy to maintain.

As your collaborative development processes mature, you will naturally start thinking about the most efficient ways to deploy and manage these macros for day-to-day use. In the next chapter, "Cloud-Based Macro Deployment," we will explore how to leverage OneDrive, SharePoint, Excel Add-ins, and Power Automate to distribute and schedule your automation tasks in a truly cloud-centric environment. This will ensure that not only is your code well-coordinated, but your deployment model remains scalable and accessible to every user who needs it.

5.   Cloud-Based   Macro Deployment

Deploying Excel automation in a cloud-centric environment offers significant advantages for both end users and the teams responsible for maintaining these solutions. One of the most accessible ways to begin is by distributing macro-enabled workbooks through OneDrive or SharePoint, allowing collaborators to open and run the files without juggling multiple versions. Storing your work in these online repositories ensures that changes are saved in real time, reducing the risk of version conflicts and promoting transparency across the organization. This approach is especially beneficial in distributed setups, where team members may need immediate access to macros regardless of their physical location or local device constraints.

Beyond simply sharing files, Excel Add-ins (XLAM) provide a powerful method to centralize and manage macros across an enterprise. By wrapping your VBA code into an add-in, you can install it on multiple workstations, giving each user access to the same library of functions without manually importing modules into every workbook. This approach not only standardizes the macros your organization relies on but also simplifies the process of rolling out updates. Instead of distributing new copies of each macro, you can simply push a revised version of the add-in. Team members then benefit from the latest improvements without needing to replace individual workbooks or re-download older files.

Office Scripts benefit from this same cloud-centric model but extend it in a modern, web-based way. Publishing scripts in Excel for the web allows you to share them just as easily as you would share a document link. Once a script is added to a shared workbook, colleagues can run it or modify it directly in their browsers, streamlining both collaboration and version control. This is particularly useful for organizations that are already invested in the Microsoft 365 ecosystem, leveraging services like SharePoint and OneDrive to host spreadsheets and automate data workflows. As scripts are stored online, rolling back to a previous version or branching off a prototype to build new features becomes a more fluid process for teams.

Hands-free operation of Office Scripts becomes possible through integration with Power Automate, which lets you schedule and trigger scripts based on specific events. For instance, you can set an automated process to run at a designated time each day or fire it when a particular row is added to a SharePoint list. This removes the need for manual intervention, particularly important for large-scale or repetitive tasks that need to be reliably executed on a regular schedule. Linking scripts with other Microsoft and third-party services broadens their scope, enabling you to automate end-to-end processes that might have previously required multiple layers of manual intervention.

As you expand your Excel automation efforts, it becomes increasingly important to ensure that your solutions perform efficiently under demanding conditions. In the next chapter, "Performance Optimization for Large Data and Files," we will explore strategies for writing lean VBA code, minimizing Office Script workbook calls, and handling massive data sets without slowing Excel to a crawl. This will help you confidently scale your automation projects to meet the most intensive business requirements.

6. Performance Optimization for Large Data and Files

Handling large data sets and sizable files in Excel requires a careful approach to coding and resource management. Even small inefficiencies can become pronounced when your workbooks contain tens of thousands of rows or files reach multiple megabytes in size. One of the most effective ways to keep VBA running smoothly is to bypass unnecessary operations, such as repeatedly selecting ranges before performing an action. Instead of relying on .Select, reference cells and ranges directly, reducing overhead and enabling your code to run in a more streamlined manner. Another beneficial strategy is to copy data into arrays in memory before processing, rather than working cell by cell within Excel. This approach dramatically cuts down on the back-and-forth between VBA and the worksheet, resulting in faster scripts and fewer performance bottlenecks.

Beyond these coding patterns, it is wise to disable features that are not immediately needed while your macro is running. Turning off automatic calculation and screen updating can free up system resources, allowing Excel to focus on executing your macro as quickly as possible. Once your code finishes performing the necessary tasks, you can re-enable these features to restore Excel's interactive functionality. This basic yet powerful tactic can make a marked difference in execution times, especially when dealing with iterative processes over large ranges of cells.

On the Office Scripts side, minimizing workbook calls is key to efficiency. Each time you read from or write to a workbook within a script, Excel for the web has to orchestrate communication with the cloud. Reducing these calls by structuring your script to gather or modify data in chunks helps you avoid unnecessary round trips. This can be achieved by batching operations or caching data locally within the script, then committing changes to the workbook in a single go whenever possible. Much like in VBA, the fewer interactions you have with the underlying spreadsheet, the better your performance will scale.

When it comes to real-world scenarios, a thoughtful blend of these practices often proves most effective. Large data sets may need chunking strategies or temporary tables to handle computations without exhausting memory or time limits. Arrays and dictionaries become particularly valuable for storing and manipulating data in memory. Designing your scripts to handle failures gracefully also helps prevent slowdowns. For example, using error handling or time checks can prevent your automation from getting stuck in an infinite loop when working through thousands of rows. These careful considerations can mean the difference between a macro that grinds Excel to a halt and one that completes its job unnoticed by the user.

Once you have refined your solutions for speed and reliability, you can confidently integrate Excel into more complex business workflows. In the next chapter, "Integrating Excel with Workflows and Other Office Apps," we will see how VBA and Office Scripts can be used to automate multi-step processes. From driving Word mail merges or sending Outlook emails to leveraging Power Automate for streamlined Teams and SharePoint workflows, this deeper integration can unlock powerful end-to-end solutions that span multiple tools and domains.

7. Integrating Excel with Workflows and Other Office Apps

Integrating Excel with broader workflows and other Office applications can dramatically expand the utility of your spreadsheets. Rather than viewing Excel as a standalone tool for storing data and running isolated macros, you can harness VBA and Office Scripts to create solutions that span the entire Microsoft 365 ecosystem. This approach allows you to leverage each application's strengths, knitting them together into cohesive processes that save time, reduce errors, and give your organization a more streamlined workflow. Yet achieving this level of integration requires more than just technical know-how; it demands a strategic perspective on how your tools can interact, how data should flow, and what your ultimate goals are for automation.

One classic application of VBA in a multi-step workflow involves using Excel data to drive mail merges in Word. For instance, you might maintain a spreadsheet of client information, and at certain intervals, you need to generate personalized letters or invoices for each client. Rather than manually copying and pasting data, VBA can serve as the orchestrator, opening the Word document, feeding it the required values, and iterating through rows in your spreadsheet. This automation transforms what could be an hours-long, error-prone routine into a simple click of a button. It also preserves a level of flexibility, since you can modify the Word template independently, adjust the data columns in Excel as needed, and rely on your VBA script to handle the rest.

Another powerful VBA-based workflow involves Outlook, where macros can automate the sending of emails tailored to specific recipients or conditions. You could, for example, query a data table in Excel to identify overdue accounts and then programmatically compose messages in Outlook that gently remind clients to settle their balances. In a more advanced scenario, your VBA script could attach the relevant documents, populate each email with personalized greetings, and even log the communication status back into Excel for record-keeping. This kind of bidirectional communication showcases how VBA can turn Excel into a command center for orchestrating not just spreadsheets, but documents, messages, and the processes surrounding them.

Office Scripts, by contrast, thrive in cloud-based workflows, particularly when combined with Power Automate. Instead of interacting with desktop applications through COM or other local interfaces, your scripts can tap into Teams, SharePoint, or Outlook via web-based connectors. If, for example, your team uses Excel Online to capture sales information, you can build an Office Script that triggers whenever new data is added to the workbook. With the help of Power Automate, that script might push updates to a SharePoint list, post notifications in a Teams channel, or file documents in a specific folder. This replaces the need for manual copying or complex local setups, making it easier for globally distributed teams to stay aligned.

Some workflows are best showcased through end-to-end examples, such as generating invoices or aggregating data from multiple forms. In the case of invoicing, Excel can maintain a list of products, customer details, and pricing structures, with a macro or script responsible for transforming these raw data points into fully formatted documents. Office Scripts shine in scenarios where that invoice then needs to be stored in a cloud location, emailed to the customer, and tracked in a system for future reference. If your organization uses SharePoint to manage client relationships, this entire process can run automatically whenever new entries appear in a form, ensuring that no invoice gets lost in the shuffle.

Excel integration does not stop at static documents, either. Automation can facilitate a dialogue between Excel and applications like Teams, enabling real-time updates for users who depend on data-driven messages to guide their tasks. This can be particularly useful for process tracking or status updates, where an entire department might benefit from being notified the moment a certain condition is met in Excel. At a more advanced level, you can design scripts to listen for triggers outside of Excel altogether, responding to events in other services that then prompt data collection or transformation in the spreadsheet. The key principle is to recognize that Excel becomes a node in a larger network, rather than a lone application cut off from essential workflows.

After exploring how Excel can integrate with other Office apps to create fully automated business processes, the next logical step is to look at how these techniques can be leveraged for reporting and dashboards. In the following chapter, "Automated Reporting and Dashboard Generation," we will examine how macros and Office Scripts can gather data from various sources, build pivot tables and charts, and generate polished outputs such as PDF reports or refreshed online dashboards. This focus on visualization and distribution closes the loop on automation, delivering insights that stakeholders can use to make informed decisions, all without burdening users with repetitive manual tasks.

8. Automated Reporting and Dashboard Generation

Building powerful, automated reporting and dashboard solutions in Excel allows organizations to transform raw data into actionable insights without placing an extra burden on users. One of the most popular methods involves writing a macro that gathers data from multiple sources, whether these reside in different worksheets, external databases, or even web-based services. Rather than forcing analysts to copy and paste information manually, a well-crafted VBA procedure can pull everything together and perform the necessary transformations behind the scenes. These automations are especially valuable for recurring tasks, such as monthly or quarterly reporting cycles, where consistency and speed are paramount.

One of the strengths of Excel for reporting lies in its robust features for summarizing and visualizing data, particularly through pivot tables and charts. A macro can set up or refresh these pivot tables automatically, ensuring that new rows of data are integrated without any user intervention. This not only streamlines workflows but also helps maintain data accuracy, since manual steps can introduce mistakes over time. Once the macros complete their refresh processes, they can generate a variety of deliverables. Commonly, organizations produce PDF reports for easy distribution, reducing the potential for accidental edits or miscommunication. Alternatively, macros can save workbooks in a template format, ready to be presented with minimal user interaction.

Office Scripts extend the capabilities of reporting and dashboard generation into a browser-based environment. Rather than storing your automation logic locally, you can run scripts directly in Excel for the web, refreshing online dashboards with the latest data. This is particularly useful for teams that rely on cloud-based workflows, as they can share dashboards in real time and trust that everyone is looking at up-to-date information. Additionally, scripts can send notifications to stakeholders via tools like Microsoft Teams or Outlook, closing the loop by alerting relevant parties that the latest numbers are ready for review. In fast-paced environments where rapid decision-making is critical, shaving minutes or hours off the reporting cycle can have a substantial impact on business outcomes.

A common example of how these techniques come together is the monthly report automation process. Suppose your organization needs a consolidated view of sales figures from multiple regions. By centralizing data in Excel, you can design a macro or Office Script that aggregates information from each regional sheet or database, cleans and transforms it, and then displays the resulting insights in pivot tables or interactive charts. Through the use of templates and consistent naming conventions, these operations run with a single click or scheduled trigger, sparing your team the repetitive labor that would ordinarily accompany each reporting cycle. The end result is a professional, consistent report every month, delivered faster and with fewer opportunities for error than manual procedures.

Once you have a reliable system for automated reporting and dashboards, it becomes critical to think about protecting the integrity of your work and maintaining compliance with organizational policies. In the next chapter, "Security and Compliance in Excel Automation," we will examine measures that safeguard your macros and scripts from unauthorized access, discuss how digital signatures and Trust Center options function in Excel, and look at security best practices for Office Scripts in the cloud. By implementing these precautions, you can ensure that even as your automations reach across your organization, they remain secure, trustworthy, and aligned with IT standards.

9. Security and Compliance in Excel Automation

Security and compliance play a vital role in any Excel automation strategy, ensuring that your organization's sensitive information remains protected and that your automated workflows adhere to internal policies as well as external regulations. One of the first lines of defence lies in Excel's Trust Center, a collection of settings that govern how macros are handled. Configuring these options allows you to define under what circumstances Excel will execute VBA code, such as enabling macros only when they are digitally signed or come from a trusted location. By carefully selecting the appropriate level of macro security, you strike a balance between openness for day-to-day tasks and protection against potential threats.

Digital signatures, which can be added to VBA projects, provide a higher level of assurance that the code originates from a reputable source and has not been tampered with. When a macro is digitally signed, Excel will recognize the certificate and display trust prompts that reflect the authenticity of the signature. Users in your organization can then verify that the macro is legitimate, supporting more confident adoption of automated solutions. This approach also aligns with IT policies in many organizations that require macros to be signed, especially when they have access to critical data or integrate with sensitive systems. While it takes some initial overhead to set up a certificate infrastructure and train developers to sign their macros, the payoff in security and credibility is well worth the effort.

Restricting macro access is another essential element of a sound security strategy. By protecting your VBA code with a password or locking the VBA project, you prevent unauthorized parties from editing or even viewing the scripts.

This measure not only safeguards intellectual property, such as proprietary algorithms or business logic, but also reduces the risk of internal threats or simple mistakes. Team members who have legitimate reasons to modify the code can be granted access to the password-protected project, while others can still run the macros without ever seeing the underlying code. This division of roles and privileges helps to maintain an environment where automation can be safely adopted across various departments.

Office Scripts introduce a different security context from traditional VBA macros, as they run in the cloud under the user's credentials. When a user executes an Office Script, it operates within the permissions assigned to that user's Microsoft 365 account. This means that any restrictions or rights enforced by the organization's Azure Active Directory policies directly govern what the script can access or modify. It also implies that users are not blindly trusting an unknown file; they can see precisely who authored the script, where it is stored, and when it was last modified. This transparent approach aligns naturally with cloud-first security principles, leveraging centralized management and logging to keep track of script activities.

From a compliance standpoint, automating tasks with Excel scripts may necessitate additional oversight, especially in regulated industries where data residency and audit trails are a concern. Because Office Scripts log execution details through the Microsoft 365 platform, administrators can review script history, see who ran a script, and confirm that the script adhered to organizational boundaries. For VBA, logging and auditing can be more piecemeal, involving event logs or custom-coded solutions that track activity. The important takeaway is that whether you favour VBA or Office Scripts, ensuring that your security measures and audit capabilities fit the compliance demands of your industry is an integral part of effective automation.

Securing and signing macros, restricting unauthorized access, and leveraging built-in cloud controls are essential steps toward a culture of confident automation. They help bridge the gap between the power of Excel-based solutions and the safeguarding of proprietary or sensitive information. In the next chapter, "Case Studies: Real-World Business Solutions," we will examine how these security considerations come into play during actual implementations. Through a series of in-depth examples, you will see how finance teams, cloud-first adopters, and enterprises handling large-scale reporting can combine robust security practices with advanced automation to achieve seamless, compliant workflows.

10. Case Studies: Real-World Business Solutions

Three in-depth case studies demonstrating advanced automation:

Case 1: Finance Team Workflow – *Version-controlled VBA macros and Office Scripts coordinate to consolidate departmental budgets from multiple Excel files into a master report, illustrating collaboration and cloud-sharing techniques.*

Coordinating a finance team's budgeting process across multiple Excel files often leads to challenges in version control, data consistency, and timely reporting. In this scenario, a company has numerous departmental spreadsheets that must ultimately feed into a master report, and the goal is to ensure that the entire operation runs smoothly without conflicting changes or outdated figures. One effective strategy involves pairing VBA macros with Office Scripts in a structured workflow, using version control systems to keep all participants aligned. This approach leverages traditional VBA macros for desktop users who handle local budget sheets, while also incorporating Office Scripts for cloud-based sharing and real-time collaboration. By carefully managing how each team member edits and updates the files, the organization can ensure that every budget input is accounted for and consolidated correctly in the final report.

Many finance teams begin by storing their VBA macros in a shared repository, such as Git or SharePoint, to facilitate controlled changes. This version control setup allows the macros to evolve over time, with developers checking in updates and rolling back if issues arise. When departmental leads open their budget spreadsheets, they can run the VBA macros to validate their numbers or apply standardized formatting before uploading them to a central location. On the cloud side, Office Scripts can be configured to perform complementary tasks like merging newly uploaded files or notifying relevant stakeholders through Microsoft Teams that fresh data is available. This interplay between desktop-bound VBA procedures and online Office Scripts ensures that changes made at each stage are recognized, tracked, and integrated seamlessly.

Cloud-sharing techniques play a major role in keeping the entire process transparent and efficient. Because not every finance team member may have experience with a dedicated version control platform like Git, using SharePoint or OneDrive can sometimes be more straightforward. Departmental budget owners simply store their files in a designated folder, and Office Scripts can be triggered to check for updates. Once new data appears, the scripts can run transformations, combine figures with existing numbers in the master workbook, and notify the macro developers if any discrepancies or conflicts need attention. By bridging these two worlds—local Excel for comfort and advanced scripting in the cloud for real-time coordination—the finance team gains a robust solution that capitalizes on each technology's strengths.

One key nuance is determining which parts of the process belong in VBA macros and which are best handled by Office Scripts. Heavy data manipulation or specialized logic might be quicker to implement in VBA, especially for team members already adept at Visual Basic for Applications. On the other hand, tasks that require cloud collaboration or tie into Microsoft 365 services, such as sending notifications to a Teams channel, are more efficiently managed by Office Scripts. In some organizations, a few advanced users maintain both the macros and the scripts in parallel, ensuring that the overall system stays functional even if certain team members prefer one method over the other. The end result is a more cohesive and resilient process, where the final master report reflects accurate, up-to-date budget data from every department without incurring the usual headaches of manual consolidation.

Case 2: Cloud-First Automation – *An Office Script + Power Automate solution that replaces a legacy VBA process, showing how to schedule data refreshes and email alerts entirely through cloud services.*

Replacing a legacy VBA process with an Office Script and Power Automate flow can radically change how organizations handle routine tasks such as data refreshes and email notifications. Instead of relying on a desktop-bound macro that may require a specific machine or user to run, cloud-first automation makes it possible to schedule operations from anywhere. A typical setup involves storing an Excel workbook in OneDrive or SharePoint, where the relevant data resides. From there, an Office Script can be written to update, transform, or validate this data. Power Automate picks up the baton, allowing you to schedule that script to run at regular intervals or trigger it based on specific events. In this way, the entire process lives in the cloud, eliminating dependencies on local configurations and creating a more resilient framework for ongoing tasks.

One option for the schedule is to set a simple recurrence, such as running the Office Script every morning at a fixed time. This works best when you have predictable data intake schedules or a defined window in which new information appears. Another approach leverages events, such as the arrival of fresh data in a connected data source or the submission of a form that populates the Excel workbook. By tying the script's execution to these triggers, you ensure that the workflow responds dynamically to actual changes, which can be especially valuable when time-sensitive actions like email alerts are needed. Both of these scheduling methods have their advantages, but they also come with different consequences. Fixed schedules might waste resources if no meaningful changes happen at certain intervals, while event-driven flows may require more complex configurations and an understanding of the underlying triggers.

Sending email notifications through Power Automate also opens up multiple choices. Some teams prefer to send a consolidated summary to a shared mailbox, giving everyone a quick snapshot of the latest updates. Others design the workflow to target individuals based on their role, delivering personalized messages or urgent alerts that prompt immediate action. Opting for a single shared mailbox keeps communication more centralized, but it can also lead to noise if too many notifications are directed to the same place. On the other hand, routing emails based on user profiles demands more upfront planning, since the automation must know who to notify under specific conditions, but it can drastically improve responsiveness by ensuring the right people see the right information at the right time.

Embracing a cloud-first mindset means the organization must be comfortable with data residing in online repositories and with scripts that run under user credentials in Microsoft 365. While this transition typically yields greater agility and reduces the burden on local machines, it also calls for robust security measures and clear IT policies. Some organizations have a straightforward approval process for cloud-based automation, while others impose stricter governance to ensure compliance and protect sensitive data. Both models are viable, yet each has its own implications for operational agility and how widely these cloud services can be adopted. By weighing these considerations, teams can make informed decisions on how to replace their older VBA workflows with solutions that tap into the modern capabilities of Office Scripts, Power Automate, and the broader Microsoft cloud ecosystem.

Case 3: Enterprise Reporting at Scale – *A hybrid approach where heavy data crunching is done with a VBA add-in for performance, and results are pushed to SharePoint where an Office Script formats and distributes an Excel online dashboard.*

Enterprise reporting at scale often presents unique challenges that require both robust data processing and seamless distribution to large audiences. One way to meet these demands is through a hybrid approach, where a custom VBA add-in handles computationally intensive tasks on desktop Excel for optimal performance, and the results are then pushed to a SharePoint location. From there, an Office Script can take over, formatting the newly updated workbook and distributing it as an online dashboard to stakeholders. This design leverages the best qualities of each technology: the raw power and familiarity of desktop Excel for data crunching and the cloud's reach for rapid sharing and real-time collaboration.

Deciding which parts of the workflow remain on the desktop and which are offloaded to the cloud requires a thoughtful appraisal of system constraints and user needs. Some teams opt to keep all computation local, citing complex reference libraries or advanced features not fully supported in Excel for the web. Others choose to push as much as possible online, focusing on reducing the overhead of local installations and making updates accessible to geographically dispersed teams. Each decision leads to different trade-offs in performance, security, and user convenience. Retaining more logic in a VBA add-in ensures that mature, specialized processes continue to run without disruption, while handing off responsibilities like dashboard rendering to an Office Script can minimize friction for end users who only need to view or interact with the final output.

Once the dashboards are posted to SharePoint, it becomes a matter of defining how and when they are refreshed. Some organizations rely on a regular schedule, allowing the VBA add-in to perform calculations overnight before triggering the Office Script to publish the updated results at the start of each workday. Others prefer on-demand updates, letting analysts or business stakeholders run the process whenever new data arrives. A scheduled approach fosters predictability and reduces the burden on busy end users, whereas an on-demand model offers more flexibility but may place additional demands on the team managing the add-in and scripts. The key is aligning these operational decisions with how often the data actually changes and how quickly managers need to see new figures.

When dealing with enterprise-scale reporting, it is also important to ensure that these hybrid workflows adhere to organizational policies and do not generate confusion among users. Some companies maintain explicit guidelines on storing data in the cloud, the specific permissions required for each site, and the chain of approval for releasing automation tools. Others are more relaxed, letting individual departments experiment and adopt best practices organically. Each governance model shapes how quickly solutions can evolve and how widely they can be shared. Smaller teams may appreciate agile freedom, while large enterprises often need more structured oversight to guarantee compliance and consistency.

Successfully implementing such a hybrid approach lays the groundwork for broader adoption of Excel automation, but it also raises the question of how best to manage and govern these macros at scale. In the next chapter, "Managing and Governing Macros at Scale," we will explore the role of IT professionals in creating an environment where these solutions thrive across the organization. We will discuss forming an automation center of excellence, conducting code reviews, maintaining a central repository of trusted macros and scripts, and training users to handle security responsibly. By taking these steps, enterprises can cultivate a sustainable ecosystem of automated workbooks that deliver value while remaining secure and well-coordinated.

11. Managing and Governing Macros at Scale

Managing and governing macros at scale demands a structured approach that balances innovation, security, and the practical needs of end users. One way to achieve this is by establishing an "automation center of excellence," which serves as a guiding body for all Excel-related automation initiatives within the organization. Such a team can oversee best practices, conduct formal code reviews, and offer support for departments that lack the specialized skills to maintain or troubleshoot macros and scripts on their own. By setting clear standards and providing resources like template scripts and documentation, organizations can reduce redundant effort and encourage employees to reuse proven solutions rather than reinvent them each time.

Another important consideration is how to maintain a repository of approved macros and Office Scripts. Some organizations choose to host everything on a version control platform like Git, providing extensive visibility into code histories and a structured process for merging updates. Others use SharePoint or a similar internal portal to share only the final, vetted versions of scripts. Deciding on the right approach often depends on how comfortable the team is with version control systems and whether your IT policies favor a centralized repository for auditing and compliance. Version control can be more transparent for developers and makes rolling back changes straightforward, while a simpler shared folder may be easier for non-technical users but lacks some benefits of granular oversight. In either case, the key is to clearly define the path that macros and scripts must take before they are deemed trustworthy enough to be rolled out.

User training for macro security is equally crucial. Even the most carefully designed processes can be undermined if users are not aware of how to handle potential threats or when it is safe to enable macros. Some organizations mandate short courses that walk employees through verifying digital signatures and validating macro sources, thereby reducing the risk of malicious or unintended code being introduced into the environment. Others rely on built-in controls, such as strict Trust Center settings, forcing macros to be signed by an approved certificate. Either method works, but each comes with trade-offs. Requiring signed macros can frustrate teams that do not have an easy way to obtain certificates, while relying solely on user vigilance leaves open the possibility of mistakes. A balance that includes both technical restrictions and user awareness often provides the greatest protection with minimal disruption.

When macros number in the dozens or even hundreds, monitoring usage and performing routine maintenance can become a significant challenge. Some organizations track macro calls through Excel's built-in auditing features or third-party logging solutions, giving IT visibility into which macros are run most frequently and by whom. This data can inform decisions about code refactoring or highlight potential points of failure. Supporting such a broad range of automated workbooks also calls for clear channels of communication. Users need a straightforward way to report issues, request enhancements, or retire macros that no longer serve a purpose. In some cases, organizations opt to centralize support through the automation center of excellence, which provides consistent troubleshooting and maintenance services, while others distribute responsibility to individual departments for quicker response times. Each model has implications for how quickly updates can be rolled out and how unified the overall approach remains.

As organizations refine these practices, they often look toward the future of automation in Excel and beyond. In the next chapter, "Future Outlook: Evolving Office Automation," we will explore how Microsoft's continuing investments in Office Scripts, possible convergence with desktop Office, and emerging technologies like Python integration and AI-driven code assistance are reshaping the automation landscape. This forward-looking perspective highlights the importance of continual learning and adaptation, ensuring that today's governance strategies remain robust enough to handle tomorrow's innovations.

12. Future Outlook: Evolving Office Automation

A notable trend in the ongoing evolution of Excel automation is Microsoft's investment in Office Scripts. Although currently designed for Excel on the web, these scripts have the potential to move closer to desktop Office functionality over time. Such convergence would streamline operations, allowing users to develop and run scripts in a unified environment without having to choose between web-based or desktop tools. On the other hand, bringing web-specific features to the desktop could require adjustments in how security, storage, and certain online integrations function. This blending of ecosystems may encourage more fluid workflows across cloud and local contexts, but it also raises questions about version compatibility and the extent to which VBA will remain necessary for certain advanced scenarios.

A parallel development lies in Microsoft's inclusion of Python for Excel. By introducing this powerful programming language directly into the Excel experience, new doors open for data analysis, visualization, and machine learning tasks that were once outside the usual scope of spreadsheet automation. While some might see Python's arrival as an eventual successor to VBA for data-heavy operations, others view it more as a complementary tool that excels at specialized tasks. The choice of when to use Python versus Office Scripts or VBA often hinges on the complexity of the analysis, the familiarity of the team with a particular language, and the broader IT policies around open-source libraries. Integrating Python might demand stricter governance, especially if external packages are employed, yet it could also reduce reliance on clunky workarounds in VBA or cumbersome data exports to separate environments.

Excel Automation at Scale:
Advanced VBA and Office Scripts for Business Solutions

As artificial intelligence continues to advance, tools like Excel's formula suggestions, GitHub Copilot, and other code-generation assistants stand poised to change the way automation scripts are developed. These AI-driven helpers can expedite coding by suggesting syntax, spotting potential errors, or offering entire snippets that address common business problems. Embracing these capabilities can boost productivity and lower the barrier to entry for newcomers. Yet it also carries implications for code quality, since relying too heavily on AI suggestions may lead to over-reliance on generated code that is not thoroughly understood. For teams that prioritize maintainability and clarity, a balanced adoption strategy might be best, using AI as a prompt or guide rather than an absolute authority. This mindset encourages collaboration between human insight and machine-generated code, producing solutions that are not just quick to build but also easy to sustain.

Continuous learning remains the most effective way to keep pace with these evolving technologies. Organizations that actively encourage professional development and experimentation will be well-positioned to integrate new tools like Python or AI-based coding assistants into their existing processes. On the flip side, individuals who resist change or cling exclusively to legacy methods may find themselves constrained in a rapidly shifting landscape. The key is to recognize that every tool, from VBA to Office Scripts to Python, serves a distinct purpose, and that true efficiency arises from leveraging each in the right context. The more flexible and adaptable the approach, the more likely teams are to stay ahead in a world where Microsoft's platforms are ever-evolving.

Having surveyed these emerging trends, it becomes clear that the future of Excel automation will revolve around a blend of technologies, each tailored to specific needs while building on the foundation of the Microsoft 365 ecosystem.

In the following "Conclusion," we will recap the essential lessons from this book and underline the ways in which mastering both VBA and Office Scripts can empower your teams to deliver efficient, secure, and scalable solutions in the workplace.

Conclusion

Reaching the end of this journey, we see how both VBA and Office Scripts play a central role in Excel automation at scale. VBA has proven its worth through decades of desktop-focused development, lending itself to specialized legacy workflows, tight integration with local files, and powerful data manipulation features. Office Scripts, meanwhile, opens new possibilities for cloud-based work, offering easier sharing, modern APIs, and an environment that aligns well with organizations growing increasingly reliant on Microsoft 365. Choosing one approach over the other might depend on your existing infrastructure, skill sets, and the demands of your projects, yet a balanced mastery of both tools offers a flexibility that can transform how your teams handle repetitive tasks and complex data processes.

By learning how to design efficient macros, secure them with solid governance practices, and integrate them with the broader ecosystem of Office applications, you can save your organization immense time and reduce the likelihood of human errors creeping into critical workflows. The decision to rely on local Excel installations or to push forward with cloud-based automation carries its own ramifications. Some teams appreciate the familiarity and extensibility of VBA, while others embrace Office Scripts for cross-platform scenarios and collaborative editing. Whichever path you take, remember that the ultimate goal is to streamline work in a way that empowers users to focus on tasks that truly add value, rather than wrestling with manual procedures or wrestling with incompatible systems.

As you apply the lessons covered here, keep an eye on both current best practices and emerging trends. The world of Excel automation is in constant motion, with new features, integrations, and development paradigms appearing regularly. Remaining agile and open to further learning ensures that your automation solutions stay relevant, whether you are enhancing existing macros or embarking on new projects in the cloud. With each improvement, you will sharpen your team's capacity to deliver solutions that are not only efficient and secure, but also scalable enough to handle the evolving needs of your business.

Finally, for those eager to dive deeper into specific technical details or address any hiccups that may arise, the appendices offer targeted references. You will find side-by-side syntax examples for both VBA and Office Scripts, suggestions for troubleshooting common pitfalls, and a wealth of resources that can guide your continued exploration of Excel automation.

Appendices:

A: Quick Reference for VBA and Office Scripts Syntax – side-by-side cheat sheet (VBA vs. TypeScript examples for common tasks).

A practical understanding of syntax differences between VBA and TypeScript can save considerable time when transitioning between classic Excel macros and modern Office Scripts. In VBA, variables are declared with statements like Dim myVar As String, and scope can be managed by placing these declarations at the procedure or module level. By contrast, TypeScript uses a syntax derived from JavaScript, so variables might be declared using let or const, combined with type annotations such as let myVar: string = "Hello". This distinction affects how you structure code: VBA requires explicit scoping keywords like Public or Private for broader visibility, whereas TypeScript manages visibility more granularly through export and import statements, as well as by controlling access in classes or modules.

The way you reference the Excel object model also differs significantly. In VBA, you typically use Application, Workbook, and Worksheet objects, calling methods and properties through dot notation, for example Worksheets("Sheet1").Range("A1").Value = 10. With Office Scripts in TypeScript, you generally start with the workbook context and chain methods like workbook.getWorksheet("Sheet1").getRange("A1").setValue(10). Although the intent is similar, the TypeScript approach relies on asynchronous handling of the workbook object behind the scenes, even if it often appears synchronous in actual usage. This means Office Scripts methods return objects or promises in a way that is conceptually more modern, but can also feel unfamiliar to those used to the synchronous style of VBA.

Error handling is another area where the two languages diverge. VBA macros often rely on On Error GoTo or other statements that funnel execution to specific sections of the code if something goes wrong. TypeScript uses try/catch blocks, mirroring standard JavaScript practices, which may require additional lines of code but provide a clearer, more flexible structure for error recovery. Additionally, because TypeScript is a superset of JavaScript, you can integrate libraries and code patterns that come from the broader web development ecosystem, a degree of flexibility not readily available in VBA. This offers advanced possibilities but also demands a deeper understanding of non-Excel-related concepts, such as callbacks or the event loop.

Office Scripts ultimately run in the browser-based environment of Excel on the web, which means certain Excel features that are deeply tied to the desktop software may be unavailable or handled differently. Conversely, TypeScript code can leverage modern ES6 features, offering more robust data structures, arrow functions, and class-based designs. VBA, while powerful, is limited to the Visual Basic runtime within Excel, and certain operations, like advanced networking or API calls, require additional workarounds or references. These restrictions can inform how you decide which tool to use for a given task. For instance, if you need broad access to web services or want to integrate with Microsoft 365 connectors, TypeScript in Office Scripts may be more straightforward, whereas tasks that rely on legacy libraries or complex user forms might still benefit from VBA.

Becoming comfortable with these syntactic and conceptual contrasts is often just a matter of practice. Familiar code patterns in one language can usually be mapped to their counterpart in the other, even if the exact syntax or execution flow shifts. By retaining a mental model of which environment you are working in—desktop Excel versus browser-based Excel—you can better decide which language to employ for each scenario, ensuring that both productivity and maintainability remain at the forefront of your development process.

B: Troubleshooting Guide – common errors and odd behaviours in macros and scripts, and how to fix or work around them.

Many issues with Excel macros and Office Scripts stem from reference or compatibility problems, where a library or method that used to work suddenly stops doing so. In VBA, this might occur if a workbook loses a key reference, resulting in error messages such as "Can't find project or library." Often, reestablishing the correct reference or toggling an available alternative resolves the issue. In Office Scripts, a similar scenario arises when a method or property is not available in the current online environment, leading to runtime errors that can be confusing if you are used to the desktop Excel model. In such cases, verifying that the functionality is supported in Excel for the web is the first step to diagnosing the issue.

Another common stumbling block involves misused objects or properties, especially when converting code from VBA to TypeScript. VBA developers are accustomed to directly reading and writing values via Range.Value or by selecting cells before performing an action. In Office Scripts, the equivalent process might require a chain of method calls or a different property, and selecting cells is no longer necessary. Mixing up these approaches can lead to code that compiles but fails to run properly. A reliable way to troubleshoot these problems is to isolate each step, confirm the intended target object, and ensure that you are calling the appropriate methods for that environment.

Error handling also presents distinct challenges in each language. VBA uses constructs like On Error GoTo, which can conceal the true source of a fault if placed incorrectly or not supplemented with thorough logging. Overly broad error handlers may catch exceptions without alerting you to what actually went wrong. A better strategy is to pinpoint critical operations, then create specialized error traps that log meaningful messages or data for debugging. In TypeScript, try/catch blocks are more granular and can be wrapped around specific operations that are likely to fail, helping you narrow down the root cause more systematically. If an error still eludes explanation, sprinkling console.log statements (in the case of TypeScript) or Debug.Print calls (in the case of VBA) can reveal intermediate values that highlight the failure point.

Sometimes code behaves erratically not because it is incorrect, but because of environmental factors. In the VBA world, macros that manipulate large numbers of cells may slow down if screen updates or calculation modes remain active. Temporarily disabling these features can speed up performance and reduce flickering, but forgetting to turn them back on can confuse users who see no apparent changes after running the macro. In Office Scripts, timing can become an issue if the script makes multiple calls to the workbook too quickly, although most actions appear synchronous. In either case, stepping through the script with debugging tools and watching variable states can clarify where the bottleneck or inconsistency arises.

Permissions and security settings also rank among the most common culprits for unexpected failures. VBA macros may not run at all if Excel's Trust Center is configured to block unsigned or all macros, leading to silent failures or errors that are vague. Office Scripts can encounter similar hurdles when the user's Microsoft 365 permissions do not allow editing or when the workbook is stored in a SharePoint site with restricted access. Resolving these problems often requires cooperation with IT or understanding which user roles can grant the necessary permissions. Ensuring that both your scripts and user accounts are aligned with organizational policies can prevent a host of permissions-based frustrations.

In situations where none of the usual fixes seem to work, temporarily rolling back to a stable version of the code is often the safest option. Version control systems like Git facilitate this by tracking changes over time, so you can identify the exact point where a script started malfunctioning. If you do not use Git, simply saving iterative copies of the workbook or macro modules can help you pinpoint the moment an error was introduced. While this method may not be as elegant, it is still invaluable for quickly restoring functionality in mission-critical environments.

Ultimately, effective troubleshooting hinges on understanding each environment's particular quirks, from how it handles references and permissions to how it manages errors and performance settings. By methodically isolating issues, validating assumptions, and applying best practices for error logging, you can resolve or circumvent most of the odd behaviours that arise in Excel macros or Office Scripts.

C: *Resources* – links to Microsoft documentation and community resources for further learning (Office Dev docs, forums, etc.).

A wealth of reliable resources can help you deepen your understanding of VBA macros and Office Scripts and stay current with the latest developments. The official Microsoft documentation, particularly the Office Dev pages on the Microsoft Learn platform, provides the most authoritative guidance and often includes step-by-step tutorials, sample scripts, and interactive modules to solidify your knowledge. These official resources are regularly updated and vetted by Microsoft experts, making them the first stop for finding APIs, code references, and best practices. Beyond the docs, Microsoft maintains an active online community where developers and power users discuss challenges, share techniques, and troubleshoot issues together. This community often convenes in areas such as the Microsoft Tech Community forums and specialized channels in Teams or Yammer within larger organizations. Stack Overflow also features a significant body of questions and answers related to both VBA and Office Scripts, and it remains a go-to place for solving coding puzzles and discovering real-world tips. In addition, many seasoned professionals and Microsoft MVPs maintain blogs or YouTube channels that dive deeply into practical Excel automation scenarios, offering insights based on direct experience in corporate environments. By combining official documentation with these community-driven discussions and expert-authored content, you can stay well-informed about updates, shortcuts, and innovative ways to leverage Excel automation tools in your own projects.

Below is a list of official and community-driven resources in English, most of which receive regular updates:

Excel Automation at Scale:
Advanced VBA and Office Scripts for Business Solutions

Microsoft Learn:
Excel Office Scripts Documentation
This is the primary destination for learning Office Scripts, featuring step-by-step examples, API references, and guidance directly from the Microsoft team.

Microsoft 365 Developer Documentation
Here you will find information on how to integrate with other Microsoft 365 services, as well as detailed explanations of the platform's capabilities.

VBA Documentation:
Excel VBA Reference
This is the official documentation for Excel macros and objects, where you can learn how individual methods and properties work, along with usage examples in VBA.

Community and Forums:
Microsoft Tech Community
Microsoft's general forum, which includes dedicated sections on Excel, Office Scripts, and Microsoft 365 integrations.

Stack Overflow – Office Scripts
Stack Overflow – Excel VBA
These Q&A sections provide answers to specific, practical problems. The community is very active and responsive here.

MVP Blogs and Video Channels:
Many Microsoft MVPs (Most Valuable Professionals) maintain blogs and YouTube channels offering practical advice on VBA and Office Scripts. Although specific web addresses and channels may change, searching for terms like "Excel MVP blog" or "Office Scripts tutorial" often leads to valuable content.

Using these resources, you can stay up to date on the latest developments in Excel automation, troubleshoot unconventional issues, and explore best practices for both VBA and Office Scripts.

www.ingramcontent.com/pod-product-compliance
Lightning Source LLC
LaVergne TN
LVHW051625050326
832903LV00033B/4658